Body Alive!

Releasing God's Life through the Local Church

Nigel Juckes

Published by
Jelly Bean Books
136 Newport Road
Cardiff, CF24 1DJ

A catalogue record of this book is available
from the British Library

Printed and bound in the UK by
4edge Limited, Essex, SS5 4AD

ISBN: 978-0-9935192-7-7

To the people of St Agnes Church, Kloof, South Africa who caught the vision to be alive to God and for his kingdom.

Contents

Introduction

How fortunate to have lived in these days – seeing a church being restored and beginning to live something of the reality of what we see in the New Testament.

Yes, we have a long way to go, but the journey has begun. And the more we see, the more we long for.

Like others, I believe that what we read in the book of Acts, and what we can infer from the apostolic letters, was meant to be the starting point for the church as it learnt how to live in the authority Jesus passed to us and the equipping power the Holy Spirit shares with each believer. Each generation should have added to the understanding and sustained the life that had been given.

The great threat to the church is its tendency to become institutional and hierarchical, for its ministry to pass to a limited professional leadership, normally solitary and monarchical; and for members to be observers of religion rather than faith players in the great match of eternity.

I have served as an ordained professional for more than thirty-eight years and have had to wrestle in three different churches where I have been appointed, seeking to help them rediscover their calling in the mind of God, displayed in his Word. If only I knew earlier what I have had to work out, at times instinctively, I could have been saved much pain. I can remember one church in particular, where I had led for five years, which so discouraged me, when what was to have been a leaders' planning event became an assault on my leadership style. I was ready to leave the institution and return to the financial world from which God had called me. With hindsight, I can see that my parishioners longed for a return to the clergy-centred church where they never had to risk anything or grow up into the stature of Christ. They wanted me to do it all for them. I call the clergy-centred model the leader-as-chaplain. He or she is there to take care of all their spiritual needs while they choose to take care of the rest of their needs. The leader can play god and does not have the challenge of empowering other leaders nor of mobilising the laity and helping them all to play their part in extending the rule of God. It is a way of leading which takes the easy path, because it does not require any kind of strategic planning – nor does it require any ordering of the life of the church. The leader only has to concern himself with himself.

I hardly need to point out the other obvious failure of such a church: it is severely limited to one person's ministry – so it can have no space for mission, since all energy is focused on caring for those inside the church. And where there should have been an army being mobilised, we have some passive consumers who are never satisfied. Some of our deepest satisfaction comes when God mobilises us and enables us to fulfil our life calling. In the clergy-centred church, I make all the choices and everyone else gets what I give them. How poor is that?

And in our age, serving stops life from being only about 'me'. The gospel really is good news to this fragmented, selfish world in which we live.

I served in my last local church as leader for nearly twenty-three years and realise what a privilege it has been to be a leader among leaders who have a heart for God and his kingdom.

So I am writing down what would have helped me throughout my time as an ordained professional. I hope it helps others.

Nigel Juckes

Part One

The Church – God's Agent on Earth

I
Working with God

Luke shares a great insight in his opening words to his second book to Theophilus, the Book of Acts: 'In my first book I wrote about all that Jesus *began to do* and teach until the day he was taken up into heaven.' Here is the basis of all ministry. None of us works *for* God – not even the clergy. Nor the great social activist with his or her good works. When people work for justice or for change, they may not be working with God and may in fact be working against God. Often, when we 'rescue' a situation, we are frustrating what God is wanting to teach someone. God's thoughts are not our thoughts, and our ways are not his ways (Zondervan New International Version, 2011, Isaiah 55) (all references henceforth to this edition), no matter how good they might seem to us.

We all know that Moses tried the man-centred approach when he killed the Egyptian slave driver who was beating an Israelite. It took forty years of being dismantled by God in the wilderness, looking after problematic and stupid sheep, before Moses was ready for the great work that he had planned for him. And they were forty years during which the suffering of God's people deepened. Those who do not gather with Jesus, scatter.

I personally believe that one of the most unfortunate movements that has happened among Christians in recent years is the popularity of the 'What Would Jesus Do' bracelets. As if any of us could know what Jesus would do in this situation, in that moment. We could perhaps guess what he might do, but only Jesus would know what he would actually do. A better question would have been a prayer: What are you doing now, Jesus, in this situation? And then next: Do you want me to join in? And then: How? To run with the question alone as it stood, so easily plays into the first temptation in Eden where instead of living in a place of connection with God, I play God. I decide what God would do without checking with him. For the Christian, the initiative rests with God and not with me.

God has invited us to work with him. This is far more exciting. Paul coins the phrase 'co-workers' with God (2 Corinthians 6:1). What is clear is that God is constantly at work (John 5:17) and he gives us the privilege of sharing in his work so that we learn to act as he does, lining up our heart and mind with his, by his Spirit.

This is such a vibrant way of seeing our Christian faith. God does not just call us to follow him and then leave us to figure it all out on our own. Jesus tells us that where he is, that is where we are to be (John 12:26): 'Whoever serves me must follow me; and where I am, my servant also will be.' So we are not left to our own devices. Nor are we to act with our own strength and our own insights. The important thing is not just that Jesus is with me, *but that I am with him*! We work in tandem with him, get to see what he is doing, and he grows our faith to believe that nothing is impossible for him and we can share in it. We see him at work first hand. It does not depend on us doing it – just on being with him and playing the part he gives us to do. The yoke of Jesus is easy and his burden is light.

Ministry depends upon him and not firstly upon us. We have to learn how to follow, how to co-operate and how to let him lead us.

The Son and the Father

This is clearly the pattern which Jesus uses. Jesus tells his team: 'Very truly I tell you, the Son can do nothing by himself. He can do only what he sees his Father doing, because whatever the Father does, the Son also does.' (John 5:19).

This verse uncovers the ministry of Jesus, who became a man so that we could understand what Christians have the potential to do. He is the prototype *person of the Spirit.* This is what is possible for a human being anointed by God to do in the power of that anointing.

It would be no use to us if Jesus had come and lived a life among us that we could not live. Many choose to understand the pattern of his life only in terms of his character. We get it when Paul speaks about the character of Jesus being produced as the fruit of the Spirit. But that is only half of the deal. In the upper room Jesus tells his disciples that as the Father sent him so he is sending them – it would be perverse if we were unable to live out the life of Jesus fully. That is why Luke tells us that the gospels only speak of what Jesus began to do. Acts is a record of what he continued to do through ordinary people like you and me.

Many Christians are aware mostly of Jesus as divine – which he is. But we fail to grasp the glory of his humanity – and the significance of his self-emptying (Philippians 2). He is fully God and fully human. Unless Jesus' life on earth is a model of what you and I can do in the power and anointing of the Holy Spirit, then Jesus does not speak the truth when he tells his disciples that they would do greater things (not more things – as some wish this verse to read!) than he did. And only by believing this will that be true in our day. And only by believing this can we understand the experience of the disciples in the book of Acts – written as a testimony for our living out of the kingdom intention of God: Father, Son and Holy Spirit. How else can you explain that a person just like you and me can get rescued from a shipwreck and cure all the sick on the island of Malta (Acts 28:9)? Jesus lives on in his church. And today more than ever we need the manifest presence of God by the supernatural gifts of the Holy Spirit (1 Corinthians 12:7) for the common good, when people are seeking spiritual reality and help, or are looking into occult and pagan forces that will destroy them. Our failure to take hold of the life God has for us condemns the world God is wanting to reach through us.

If we are going to win the world for Jesus; if we are going to extend God's rule for the return of the King of kings, then we need to advance the kingdom as Jesus did, by doing what the Father is doing through the working of the Holy Spirit.

The longer ending of Mark's gospel expresses it this way: 'Then the disciples went out and preached everywhere and the Lord worked with them and confirmed his word by signs that accompanied it.' This is the pattern established when the church was born. And gospel advances when we work in God's way with him.

One of the great and stunning descriptions of what it means to be a Christian is given to us by Paul in his letter to the Galatians (2:20): 'I have been crucified with Christ and I no longer live, but Christ lives in me. The life I now live in the body, I live by faith in the Son of God, who loved me and gave himself for me.' This does not describe the experience of the new birth and new life in Jesus as a one off event. This is the reality of life now – and life and ministry run all the time because Jesus lives in us and expresses his *whole* life through us. I can today have the impact in this life in this world that Jesus had in his life in his day in his world. I do not just minister when I do it consciously. I carry the presence of Jesus, I am his temple, a place of his residence on earth now. I carry his authority and I carry his power by his Holy Spirit. Later in his Galatians letter Paul urges us to walk in step with the Spirit. That is how we keep up with what God is doing in the world with us as well as what he is doing in us to transform our character into the likeness of Jesus.

Paul came into faith with this awareness. When he met Jesus on the road to Damascus, Jesus said to him: 'Saul, Saul, why are you persecuting me?' How had he persecuted Jesus but in the lives of those in whom Jesus continued to live out the life of the Father by the presence of the Holy Spirit? When Paul persecuted them, he persecuted Jesus directly.

I love this verse in Paul's letter to the Colossians (1:29), in which Paul describes how he works at this partnership: 'To this end I strenuously contend with all the energy Christ so powerfully works in me.'

It is one hundred per cent God and one hundred per cent me together. We work out the victory and triumph of the cross, applying it in every situation and life – and as Bill Johnson puts it: 'Jesus gets what he paid for.'

Priesthood of All Believers

This is one of the glorious truths restored in the reformation of the 16th century. Unfortunately it does not seem to have changed ministry in the church until centuries later. It gave us a restored confidence to enter the presence of God with boldness. But the role of the priest is a two way movement: From God to man as well as man to God. We realised we now had the one and only mediator between us and God, the man Jesus (1 Tim 2:5), but we lost the fact that we are a kingdom of priests to the world and to one another. We recognised we did not come to God through anyone except Jesus, but we still permitted clergy to minister to the church while the church failed to take up its Body ministry. And so clergy of the reformation became a new priesthood. They were the ones who went into ministry – or 'into the church' as people used to say. All of this fixes in people's minds that only the few minister. The rest only receive. What poverty in place of the richness God intended – both for ministry and mission.

We have all the words, even in our liturgies, asserting that from baptism we have been made part of this glorious heritage. But we have neither been let in nor have we beaten on the door – or was it a ceiling? If all believers are priests, then all of us not only can come with boldness into his presence, we can go with boldness into each day to manifest his life and work through our lives. We represent him to one another and to those whom God is reaching in his world. We are an army which needs mobilising, a body needing to be raised up, stirred to life so that we can accomplish God's work in our generation.

If leaders in the church work with God to equip God's people for works of service, we could transform the world in our life time. God needs us – and is depending upon us. There is no other plan and no other is necessary, because each one of us has the potential to do what Jesus did if we are surrendered to him and his purpose. Was it Moody who heard the call in the challenge of what God could do through one man fully surrendered to him? And he said: 'I want to be that man.' If ordinary believers catch the vision for their potential in the hand of God, an army of one Christian in seven people in the world's population could win the world in our generation.

Imagine!

II
The Church, His Body

The concept of the church as the body of Christ is a popular one for Paul. It has many things which it images for us.

Basically it is a reminder that Jesus continues to live on this earth by his Holy Spirit and through us.

Luke wrote his gospel about 'all that Jesus began to do and to teach'. The account continued in Acts. And it continues in the street where you live today. Jesus still walks the earth to change the world by the power of his cross and resurrection – and we are his limbs, his tongue, his hands, his incarnate image.

His Body, the Fullness of Him Who Fills Everything in Every Way

Paul ends what is for us chapter one in Ephesians with these words (v 23). He has written down a stunning prayer which we should pray over the church frequently:

> I pray that the eyes of your heart may be enlightened in order that you may know the hope to which he has called you, the riches of

> his glorious inheritance in his holy people and his incomparably great power for us who believe.

He follows this with words about that power being the same power that raised and exalted Jesus.

It is an exaltation which is for now and for eternity – placing Jesus far above all rule, authority and dominion, with everything under his feet.

He then speaks of how God the Father appointed Jesus head over everything for the church, which is his body, the fullness of him who fills everything in every way. It is *for the Church*, at our disposal. What Jesus is and holds, he expresses through us. All this is for the church, his Body. What he is, he shares with us so that we carry the power of the cross, applying it to every situation by the power of the Holy Spirit.

From Genesis 1, we were created to rule on the earth. We abdicated that role when our first parents doubted God and instead trusted the Deceiver, yielded to that adversary of God and took with them that rule which had been entrusted to us, and the Deceiver became the prince of this world. In Adam, all die (1 Corinthians 15:22 cf Romans 5:12ff). We were born into his dominion, that of the darkness and of death. When Jesus disarmed Satan on the cross, he bought back with his blood that authority and rule which we had lost. He added it to his authority in heaven, which he had never lost. So his declaration in Matthew 28 is a declaration that he now holds again *all* authority in heaven and on earth and can bestow it on those who are part of his

Body. Those of us who turn to him in saving repentance are transferred from the dominion of darkness into the kingdom of God the Son whom the Father loves. We live into the new reality of the coming age. As the kingdom of God breaks into this world today, it is a sign of what will be when God's rule is fully restored in the new heaven and new earth.

God does not give the Spirit in measure but in fullness (John 3:34). He does not give the Son in part but in fullness. Christ is in us, the hope of glory. We are complete in him. Jesus lives fully in his Body. And just as Jesus brought heaven's reality to earth in his three years of ministry in the power of the Holy Spirit, so his present Body continues to have access to all the resources of heaven by the same Holy Spirit, because we are in Him.

We are to live by faith on earth to bring in the rule of God more and more – reaching one life at a time, one situation at a time, restoring that which has been robbed by the Thief. People are transformed by an encounter with the Lord of all, whenever Jesus acts through us, his Body.

When the Body Works, There is No Limit to What God Can Do

Ephesians 4 is a passage often turned to when the church wants to learn about leadership and the church – but it also contains the big picture of why God has ordered his Body as he has. The One who has ascended on high and has given gifts to us his people, has done it *to fill the whole universe* (v 10).

We are not just working out our salvation, we are not just working in some little field assigned to us by God. All creation is watching us with longing (Romans 8:19, 20), because the redemption of creation, which fell because of our disobedience, will ultimately be restored through our obedience to the King as we hasten the day of his return. We serve so that Jesus fills the whole universe.

So there are some assumptions in Ephesians that will make this possible:

- God's people must minister (v 12). The coming of the kingdom that we pray for daily with the words Jesus gave us (Your kingdom come on earth as in heaven!) is not going to happen with just the leaders serving. We are all to serve. We are all to risk. I only start to grow when I start to trust that Jesus can use me, and share his life through me. I don't change because I understand something. I don't change because I agree with a truth. I only change when I begin to work it. The goal for each Christian is to be a little Christ – to aspire to the whole measure of the fullness of Christ. And we only grow up into him when we work with him, becoming like him in ministry as we do his works with him.

- We will not mature on our own. The whole Body is built up when I play my part. We enrich one another and provoke one another. When someone gives a testimony of how God acted through them, I am reminded of my inheritance in Christ. *This could be me* must be the thought, as I celebrate what God has done through them. I am only the Christian I am because I belong, and am grafted deeply into, his Body. I could never be the Christian I am without everyone else. Jesus has grown me through you.

▪ But I am also responsible for you. And you are responsible for you, and me for me! I can give to you, but will you receive from me and from Jesus? The witness of the church is impoverished because, like Peter, we don't want our feet washed by Jesus (John 13). And some of us think we are not able to take the role of servant and wash the feet of others. Therefore, too often the Body looks fairly broken – and its witness in the world is not attractive to those who need what we have. But when the Body functions, the whole Body becomes increasingly a manifestation of the life of Jesus. We are healed as God uses each of us to play our part, giving and receiving life from Him. And when he is lifted up, he is able to draw all to himself.

▪ As Paul puts it, it is where we connect that life flows (v 16). The more connected I am, the more I can give and the more I can receive. This clearly puts an end to any notion that one leader can give to the Body what it needs. Or that the leader will receive what is needed from the Body, unless they are connected in some life changing way with those next to them. Those we empower to serve are able even to serve us who are set over them. Why not? I personally receive most of the ministry I need from those around me in the local church. At times I receive when I am at conferences. There has seldom been anyone hierarchically above me who has ministered to me – and I have no expectation in this regard. But I do know where to go – and I seek out what I need. We receive where we connect. And as leaders we are responsible for our own lives – the initiative to get help rests with us. We are no longer babes, nor helpless victims.

▪ All talk of Body is empty if connection is low. Before taking us into the other truths, Paul urges the church: 'Make every effort to keep the unity of the Spirit though the bond of peace.' This is such a crucial role of leadership: to model and guard the unity in the leadership team and to facilitate the unity of the whole. Seek peace – no, pursue it! If the Body is sick, it cannot function freely. And the medium is much of the message. So let's get ourselves and the church fixed and live as God intends us to do. The Body of Christ is not a human organisation – and it carries within it the resources of heaven to enable it to be whole. Let's give to each other what God gives to us, so that we can be the good news we want to share. I love the way the NIV translates v 15: 'Instead, speaking the truth in love, we will grow to become in every respect that mature body of him who is the head, that is Christ.' Here is the potential of the Body indeed. A maturity and fullness in Christ and for Christ.

This last point is underlined wonderfully in Romans 12. Paul says of the Body: 'Each member belongs to all the others.' How this confounds our individuality and the virtual worlds into which many of us disappear. I am not my own – I was bought at a great price. I belong not only to Jesus, who paid for me. I belong to each and every one of you because I am God's gift to you. But you are also God's gift to me and everyone else in his Body. To withhold yourself is to deny God and to cut yourself off from his purposes for you. In our uniqueness as persons and the uniqueness of the way his gifts are expressed through each, and because of the unique connections that we each have, no one else on earth can do what each one of us can do. I need you and you need me. And God amazingly chooses to want us too.

In Accordance with the Faith God Gives

This is another product of being in the Body and being gifted to serve. Paul instructs us (Romans 12): 'Do not think of yourself more highly than you ought, but rather think of yourself with sober judgment, in accordance with the faith God has distributed to each of you.' Your faith stirs mine, and mine yours. Your testimony provokes my faith.

Faith can be a scarce commodity in the church. Jesus continually flags this. If his disciples disappointed him in any way, it was because of their lack of faith.

And he once expressed a deep concern (Luke 18:8): 'When the Son of Man returns, will he find faith on the earth?'

God is reminding us that we have the resources of heaven to do the works of God with him. If our ministry is according to our capabilities, are we thinking of ourselves more highly than we ought?

We need a stretch – we need faith, *to live beyond ourselves*, in his enabling. If there is no risk, it is not service, and possibly sin (Romans 14:23). Moving in the gifting is to take us out of our place of comfort to see God act through us. According to his power at work within us, he is able to do more than we can ask or imagine. This is our calling and our purpose.

If Your Gift is Serving, Serve; Teaching, Teach...

The message is plain and simple. Use it or lose it. The parable of the talents is really strong on the fact that one day, as Christians, God will ask each one of us: What have you done with the grace you received? Gone are the days when we think that I'm OK, I have my ticket to heaven and I can cruise all the way home. A gospel of salvation is narrow and there is no evidence for it in the Good News Jesus brought. His was a gospel of the kingdom. When I am saved, I am saved to serve. I have turned from rebellion and surrendered and made peace with the King. I am now a soldier in his army. Jesus has now enlisted me to restore the rule of God to the earth, to apply the triumph of the cross into every life, every organisation, every home and every town, every nation.

*

Members Do Not All Have the Same Function

This almost goes without saying. As I said above, our uniqueness is part of the diversity from our creative God. Even teachers differ from each other – and God gets through to you with that person rather than this. Every gift that is needed is present – but the church is handicapped because some of those gifts have been hidden in a hole in the ground and are not growing – and they do not bless the one who has them, and they cannot bless the Body because nothing is given away. Part of the task of leadership is to give you space to offer yourself and the gifts God gives you – but you also need to offer yourself as a living sacrifice.

We need to consider what will be said of our lives. We will hear either: Well done, good and faithful servant. You have been faithful with a few things. I will put you in charge of many things. Come share your master's happiness. Or we will hear this: You wicked and lazy servant...

If the Foot Should Say: Because I am Not a Hand...

I love the imaginative way in which Paul speaks of our interdependence in 1 Corinthians 12. One of the greatest joys comes not from wishing I was someone else but in knowing who I am and how I am gifted so that I can experience the fulfilment which comes from this alone. Satan robs us and robs the Body when we allow ourselves to be distracted into wanting to be what we are not. And if we try to live someone else's life, or work outside of our gifting, it will only bring frustration and damage to us and others. And we run the danger of cutting out the person who is gifted from the place that God wants for them. So the whole Body suffers.

The foot needs the eye. The mouth needs the ear. When each plays their assigned part, then the Body is whole and functions as it was designed by God. When we withhold ourselves, the Body is crippled, it stumbles, it lacks an ability to see or hear. God's vision is for a church, a body which is alive and fully equipped and functional, to do his work on the earth.

We are the Body

The church needs to rediscover that it is the body of Christ. We refer casually to the church as the Body – even when it is so dysfunctional, even non-functional, that that is the last name we should give it. It is so easy for the church to become institutional rather than organic. There is nothing hierarchical in the Body – so anything which operates like a corporate vehicle is missing the point; more than that it will drain the Body, because it draws resources to serve itself, the structure, rather than the kingdom of God. If the leadership is not serving the life of the Body, to make it pulsate with the life of God, in time it will destroy it.

God has left us sacramental support to strengthen our unity (1 Cor 10): 'Is not the cup of thanksgiving for which we give thanks a participation in the blood of Christ? And is not the bread that we break a participation in the body of Christ? Because there is one loaf, we who are many are one body, for we all share one loaf.' Our unity is held by him. It is when we eat his flesh and drink his blood that we remain in Jesus (John 6:56) and he in us. The Body is held together in its worship of the Head, Jesus Christ. He feeds and sustains its life and unity.

And the Body is always local – it assumes connection where life flows to *and from* every member. This is not a picture to describe a denomination or a fellowship of churches. Body can only happen in one location. It can be experienced at different levels in cell, congregation and even parish – but only to the degree that we connect within each level. And where we connect, life flows among all the parts. That is the body of Christ.

III
The Potential in the Church

I sometimes dream: What if the more than one billion Christians in the church were mobilised? Would we complete the Great Commission next year? As long as the church continues to disempower every Christian and see only the professionals as the ministers, not only will the church be a feeble shadow of what it could be, but its capacity to change the world will be almost non-existent. The professionals are caught up in ministry which is essentially inward looking. And there is a limit to how many people they can handle on their own.

I believe that if leaders catch a vision for mobilising the whole church, we will release human resources into God's hands that could see God's kingdom come on earth as in heaven far sooner than has been imagined.

Holy Spirit Renewal

I realise that I have lived through a really exciting period in the history of the church. There has been a restoration of life in the church that has made our understanding of the New Testament real. We experience again now what they experienced in the time of the New Testament. As he acted then in the New Testament accounts, God still acts now. He has restored life to the church through the dynamic working of the Holy Spirit.

- Initially there was the Charismatic renewal as God restored to his church the gifts of the Holy Spirit listed in 1 Corinthians 12. These are the supernatural gifts of the Holy Spirit which God gives to the church to advance his Kingdom in power: Wisdom, Knowledge, Faith, Healing, Miracles, Prophecy, Discernment of spirits, Tongues and the Interpretation of tongues. This confounded a church that had been so overwhelmed by the rationalism of the enlightenment that it had lost its spiritual heart and identity. The church had struggles with basic beliefs such as the incarnation of God in Jesus and his resurrection from the dead – and not to have the paradigm to handle these destroys the Christian faith which rests on them. So God was restoring the church so that people in our post-modern world could find their way home to God. We are spiritual beings, made in the image of the One who is Spirit (John 4: 24). When the church stopped believing in the supernatural, we had nothing to offer seekers looking for spiritual reality with which to connect. There was a resurgence of paganism, spiritualism and spreading of eastern religion (what is called the New Age) but all of this is occult spirituality which in the end leads to demonisation and death. The purity of the Holy Spirit is the only spiritual reality which blesses us.

But more than that, these supernatural gifts are the 'tool kit' of God for mission. Read again how God used Christians in the book of Acts to manifest the reality of God through these gifts, so that people lined up to receive from the hand of God the blessings of his life.

As people rediscovered the prophetic gift, God was able to break through into the lives of unbelievers as they encountered him through a word of revelation, which made God real for them.

- After the Charismatic Renewal came a recovery of biblical ministry – accompanied by debate around whether apostles could exist in our age or whether they were limited to the era of the first century. Some led the way, and even if mistakes were made, it was because we were all in a learning curve. Those who experimented shared with those of us who watched still unsure. And churches that began to experiment with new models of leadership began to discover the importance (attested to in the Bible) of the foundational role of apostles and prophets in a church which could grow, multiply, plant in a way that pastors and teachers could never match. Danny Silk has uncovered some of this in his book *A Culture of Honour*. Mike Bickle also did some helpful work on the relationship between the apostolic and the prophetic in leadership. Something of the growth and vitality of the church owes a debt to these pioneers of restoration.

▪ The move of God through John Wimber allowed the reality of the gifting of every member to get down to where God needed it. Equipping the saints was his great theme, and he released us to minister healing in a way in which we had not been successful before. What was significant was all the charismatic gifts which came into play to accomplish the work of ministry. It was as if God put into our hands tools we had not picked up before, assuming rather that these were reserved for specialists. We had seen the Katherine Khulmans or the Francis MacNutts but we did not know this ministry was for us too. And we learned how to watch for God's move upon a person and to wait for him to minister.

▪ And then came Toronto, which moved us into a deeper awareness of the presence of God. In our own church, we found that the Holy Spirit made God so powerfully present that demons were exposed in prayer ministry in a way they had never been before. We had experienced God powerfully present in worship and in anointed evangelistic preaching, but when the Holy Spirit is honoured and given public space, he makes God's presence real in a disturbing way. And we had to learn how to set people free, which we were able to do without all the striving that had been our experience in the past. We came to understand that demons operate on rights, and rights come from sin: our sin, the sins of others to us and sins in family lines. But following repentance, forgiveness to those who had hurt us and renunciation of occult involvement and similarly damaging sexual sin, and the demons had to leave.

God's Masterpiece

In Ephesians 3:10, Paul writes that God's intent was that now, through the church, the manifold wisdom of God should be made known to the rulers and authorities in the heavenly realms according to his eternal purpose that he accomplished in Jesus Christ our Lord.

What is clear is that a powerless church is no threat to hell. But a church on the move in the anointing of the Holy Spirit, as we see with the church in the Acts of the Apostles, invading the dominion of darkness, storming the gates of hell, is a threat to be reckoned with. This is the church in God's mind. It is for this that he is restoring his church. It puts God – the powerful, proactive, victorious, triumphant conquering Lord of Revelation – on display to a world that is bored with a church that can only offer words and not reality. My prayer is that before I die I will see the church looking a lot more like the church in Acts, and even beginning to move beyond the church in Acts as people take hold of what has been restored, adding revelation of possibility to what is already expected. And we have to learn how to sustain what God has revealed and to pass it on to those who come after us, so that the kingdom comes in power and not in fits and starts.

For too many, the church before this period of restoration is what has been settled for. This is the model that feels safe. But it is a model which is impotent and lacks the life which a spiritually hungry and thirsty world is searching for. I believe God sees us as his agent for his Kingdom, and that he is longing to impact the world through each one of us as he was able to impact the world through his Son. We are to grow up into the full stature of the Son – not just in character but also his gifting, anointing and ministry. Think of the potential of the impact of one billion 'Jesus' people on earth! Because as the Father sent him, Jesus sends us (John 20: 21) with all the resources of heaven in our hands by his Holy Spirit. We will never achieve our end in isolation. It is you and I together, spurring one another on, collaborating as we go, sharing with one another what we are discovering so that together we can go much further.

Let us read the Bible and long and pray and ourselves make possible a church which derives its identity from such efforts, and not from the emasculated church which is locked inside buildings, concerned with its own life and missing God's lost world.

The 21st century is the time for the church to come into its own, using what God has restored to us to win the world for him.

IV
The Anointed Body

There is an inseparable link between, first, the release of the gifts and, second, ministry and the operation of the Holy Spirit in the church. If we want to see a priesthood of all believers, where Christians begin to move into ministry, this is not something that can be organised at some kind of human level. Many churches have tried to operate systems to get people mobilised. We cannot manufacture Body life in the church. It can only come from the One who is head and who energises us by his Holy Spirit.

What I am trying to warn of is that we cannot read a book like this and then re-organise the furniture and hope that the church will be different. It is the Spirit who distributes the gifts as he determines (1 Cor 12:11).

Many years ago Terry Fullam highlighted for me the two works of the Holy Spirit in the life of the believer. Both are prophesied in the Old Testament. They are identified by two prepositions: In and On/Upon.

The Spirit In (Ezekiel 36:25ff)
I will sprinkle clean water on you and you will be clean; I will cleanse you from all your

> impurities and all your idols. I will give you a new heart and put a new spirit in you. I will remove from you your heart of stone and give you a heart of flesh. And I will put my Spirit in you and move you to follow my decrees and be careful to keep my laws.
>
> **The Spirit On/Upon** (Joel 2:28f)
> And afterward. I will pour out my Spirit on all people. Your sons and daughters will prophesy. Your old men will dream dreams and your young men see visions. Even on my servants, both men and women, I will pour out my Spirit in those days.

The first is a work of the Spirit in the heart which will result in a new capacity to live differently from how God's ancient people have lived in the past. The new heart speaks to me of a newness of life which is evidence of being made alive in Christ (Ephesians 2:5), or born again of the Spirit (John 3:3, 5).

The second is the mark of Pentecost where, instead of just a few individuals being anointed with power from on high (as in the Old Testament: kings, prophets, etc.), all believers were so anointed. And the capacity to live out that anointing in terms of supernatural ministry is the mark of all believers living under the new covenant: 'God has made us competent as ministers of a new covenant – not of the letter but of the Spirit; for the letter kills but the Spirit gives life'

(2 Corinthians 3:6). It is by the Spirit that the kingdom comes – it is not a matter of talk but of power (1 Corinthians 4:20). It is the gifts which make God visible, manifest (1 Corinthians 12:7).

Anointing and Authority

The great commission given by Jesus in Matthew 28 is our mandate:

> All authority in heaven and on earth has been given to me. Therefore, go and make disciples of all nations, baptising them in the name of the Father and of the Son and of the Holy Spirit, and teaching them to obey everything I have commanded you (vv 19, 20).

The authority which Jesus has is the authority which was once given to us in Genesis 1:28. God created us and appointed us as his vice-regents here on earth. We were to exercise his rule and subdue the earth – to bring it into God's order, making it productive. That authority was lost by us in the Fall, when we chose to play god and trust the Deceiver rather than our Creator God. So it required one man, God the Son incarnate, to come and recover what the first Adam lost. He paid with his own blood to buy back what we so carelessly lost. And with the defeat of Satan on the cross, that authority has now been recovered by Jesus and is held in his hands to give back to us who come under his Lordship. So any kingdom ministry is the application of the fruit of the cross into lives and situations in the power of the Spirit. That is the authority we carry.

And it is the use of this authority which is the fundamental discipleship which we must pass on to those who respond in faith to Jesus.

It took me many years to understand what John Wimber had been saying. What we must teach the new disciples to do is 'to do the stuff'. Because we must keep alive the mission of the church the way Jesus did. The 'commandments' which Jesus is referring to here are not those which enjoin us to Love our enemies, Love our neighbour, and Love God. They are the *missional* commands. It is these that we must teach them to obey: Heal the sick, raise the dead, cleanse the lepers, cast out demons and preach the Good News. These are the cutting edge things – they are the things that catch a generation that no longer wants to know if something is true. They want to know: Does it work? Yes it does. Is it real? Manifestly. Jesus lives his gospel life through us. We carry his authority and we carry his powerful anointing. We can heal the sick, cleanse the lepers and cast out demons…

And it is only when we keep these as our default setting that we will continue to experience the anointing. You see, if I never seek to bring healing, then I can go on living with the limitations of my own life, my natural giftings. But if I seek to put God on display through an exercise of the supernatural gifts, then I keep having to wait on him and invite his presence to transform this person and then that. As we drink from him, so rivers of living water flow from us. We learn how to deepen our dependence upon him. It is about a lifestyle of anointing and ministry that we learn to live in.

Anointed Body

Any Christian who has been at some combined church gathering will have heard Psalm 133 quoted. Yes: when God's people live together in unity, there the Lord bestows/commands his blessing of life. But the picture is of oil coming down from the head (Jesus) on to the body. It is in our unity that the anointing flows down. In a kingdom culture the flow of the anointing reaches right down to the feet. We learn by watching and then doing. We will never be as effective on our own – or only a few will shine. But as a team, as Body, we can all get to shine, from the most prominent and visible to the least seen. It is in the anointed Body that a culture of the kingdom can be sustained. On our own, it is unsustainable. And a Body which is fragmented and unconnected cannot carry nor experience the blessing of God promised by this Psalm.

Part Two

Leading the Movement

V

The Leader is Key

Although I understand that the best leadership, and certainly New Testament model for biblical leadership, is always plural, in the system which most of us understand or have inherited, there is the one senior person who is *primus inter pares* (first among equals). Whatever his or her title, more than anyone they have the capacity to affect the way in which the church operates. They can either unlock the potential of the Body or frustrate its purpose. So this chapter is addressed to that key person. If they continue to operate in isolation the church is at risk, and in my opinion, so are they. But if they learn to gather a team of leaders with them – and submit to them, as those leaders submit to him or her – the church is not only safe, it's potential can flourish.

In our own church, it is the team of senior leaders, the elders, who see the whole picture. In a church which has a complexity, with a variety of leaders leading elements of the life, not every leader knows all the others nor what ministry God is doing in every part of the church's life. But at an eldership level, it is held together and it is our job to make sure that where people need to collaborate, they do. And the senior person is the one who more than most needs to see the whole – and to be free from the particular hands-on leadership of a particular ministry, to assess and address the gaps, motivate where effort needs to be put, and so on.

What Ministry Does Not Depend upon Me?

I think one of the most crucial questions any senior leader needs to ask is: When I leave this church, what ministry will remain in this place? Where the leader plays the role of chaplain to the church (see Introduction) or has a controlling personality which cannot release others to take responsibility, when the senior leader dies or leaves, most, if not all the ministry leaves too. It is essentially a 'senior-leader-centred church', rather than a Jesus-centred church.

When the senior person leaves, if the only gap left is that of someone who leads the elders, but every other function of the church is covered and can continue to work with relatively little stress for those elders, then that leader has achieved their call, which is to equip and empower the whole church. As Christian Schwartz (*Natural Church Development* materials) makes clear, there is a world of difference between an empowered leader and an empowering leadership.

We have been aware of the words addressed to leaders in Ephesians 4 since God began his current restoration of the church in the 1960s/70s. The leadership of the apostle, the prophet, the evangelist, the pastor and teacher are there *to equip God's people for works of service.* It is their leadership which enables the Body to become the Body. Leadership equips and empowers and releases the ministry of the church. That is one of the chief roles of church leadership.

I find that people really struggle just to lead! By that I mean that we think that unless we are hands on, we are not ministering. But leadership itself *is a ministry* that is essential for the strengthening of the church. We who have been hands on, in time need to be those who mentor and grow others to take the ministry we once did, and to take it way beyond where we took it. Leadership is the gift given by God to make the church effective. We have wisdom and insight from such close involvement, so we know the problems and issues people are working on. But times change and people change. It is younger people and newer Christians who are closer to the culture from which people are coming into the church, and they need to be finding solutions for the lives of those cared for in their own generation. So if the church is to thrive in a rapidly changing world, older leaders must hand on to younger ones.

So we lead the leaders who lead the ministers – and minister to them to make them more effective because they have someone to reflect with. This is a glorious and crucial calling, and I hope that more people will be prepared to pay the price of leading so that many more people find a space for the fulfilment of their God-given potential.

A good elder helps a leader to be a better leader. My task is to take the person 'out of the engine room and up on to the bridge'. As elder, I am there to help them to look at what is happening in their ministry team, help them to see the gaps and opportunities, help them to discover solutions to challenges they face. We need to model the leadership that we want leaders to pick up and run with. More than anything, we need to help leaders to be empowering. There is nothing worse than allowing someone to take on the leadership of some aspect of the church's life and then find that they have done all the work themselves. At our church we did not appoint anyone as a paid staff member to do the ministry - but we employed them to facilitate more opportunities for members to volunteer. The ministry is carried by the volunteers – and the more the better! So when, for example, our pastoral team wanted to *employ* a pastor to handle things like crisis visits to hospitals, the leadership refused to do this. Such a person would take ministry away from those in the Body gifted to care. And those who believe they have not been visited or cared for unless the senior leader calls are helped to understand that they get better care from someone gifted and anointed to care than from a professional who can only do it professionally, and often is unavailable, and certainly cannot commit to a regular weekly visit – or even more frequently in times of crisis. This way of doing things is far more supportive because that person with a pastoral gift is devoted to this ministry and fulfilled by what they offer. Willowcreek Church has discovered that the pastoral gift is the most widespread in the Body. So why expect the leader with a title or position to do what they may not even be gifted to do? If they have such a gift, then strategically that gift should be deployed at the highest level to care for and grow the key leaders.

Ministry to the Leader

There are a number of things which God has done in my life

which have helped me to be a more effective leader.

- **Identity:** How crucial that the leader is a person who is secure in who they are. And as Christians we have the best of this. We have an identity as adopted children of our Heavenly Father, through Jesus our Saviour. This is something God has done. It has nothing to do with our suitability, or some other qualification in us. It is the fruit of his love for us – and he adopted us in his Son. The commitment of God to you and to me is far greater than our commitment to him. He has taken us on for eternity. We are his; we are beloved and we are safe. At its core, I have a personal faith in God which is not dependent upon me but on him.

  This secure sense of identity needs to be addressed if I am not to destroy myself, those around me and the church. When I am not secure, those around me are not free. They cannot question things, they cannot criticise, they cannot help the church to be better because I, the leader, frustrate anything that God wants to do because I am too busy guarding me rather than releasing the church. This is a particular work of the Holy Spirit who is sent into our hearts, enabling us to cry 'Abba, Father', God's Spirit testifying to our spirits that we are indeed his child. I belong to him and he has my back.

  I know that when I am most insecure because of events or people who have unsettled me, because of criticism which I am struggling with or betrayal by those alongside me in leadership (and we all go through these things, because leaders are in the line of fire in the church from within and without), what I need most of all is to get my relationship with God uncluttered. I need to know again that I am his and he is mine. I need to know that his love for me is unaffected by what I have done. He knows the worst and still loves me, fully and completely and without reservation. His love is not dependent upon how lovable I am. It rests upon the fact that love is his essential nature. Even his judgment is shaped by his love.

- **Whole:** Connected to the above – and at times hindering us from experiencing it fully – are all the unresolved issues in my life. If we have a problem with authority figures, we need to get it healed. We cannot exercise authority if we cannot accept it from others. If we have unhealed hurts from relationships, we will become those who hurt others. If we have been abused (and what leader has not had a good share of abuse from those led?), we will only be free to bless the church when we have been helped to a place of forgiveness of those who hurt us so that we can love them too.

Too many churches suffer from older leaders who bear a whole list of unhealed wounds, some of them dating way before their calling. It is too easy to move into ministry out of the place of our own needs – and to seek to address my needs by meeting needs in others. We live in a whole lot of unwholesome co-dependent relationships with needy people whom we cannot help because we need them to remain needy.

Don't you love the account of the restoration of Peter after the resurrection? They meet Jesus at the sea of Galilee and Jesus asks Peter three times about his love. You see, if Peter does not love Jesus freely, if Peter does not know himself to be forgiven for the damning work of denial, he will never be free to serve. Instead, he will always be seeking to prove to Jesus – and everyone else – just how sorry he was. But that is no motivation to serve. The only way to serve others is out of the free love of Jesus himself and knowing ourselves beloved.

Jesus had to face into these issues when he was tempted by the Devil before he began his public ministry. I have just mentioned above the first temptation: it is to feed off the ministry when I need to be needed by you. My needs feel comforted as I meet your needs. Then there is the temptation to be the showman – it is all about image, about what people see rather than what is in the heart. But this is a deathly ministry because it is only out of the depths of our own experiences and our vulnerability in sharing them, that we are able to reach into the depths of those we serve. The more superficial my leadership, the more phony the church. And then there is the ability to handle power. In the kingdom of God it is power to empower. But when we need power for self, when we need to be in control, when we need to be the one to whom everyone looks, we have lost the plot.

Good leadership is in some ways actually invisible. Foundations are not things that you see when you look at a building. That is the role of the apostle and prophet. People can look at the building and know that it has strong foundations. They can look at the church and immediately know it is being well led – because it is not the senior leader who is on display, but Jesus who is manifested every place the gifts are operating. The more the gifts, the more Jesus shows himself.

So the church is a healing community. This is the place where I get fixed. I do not have to go to some other place, to some expert. The gifts needed are here among my brothers and sisters – and perhaps one of the greatest testimonies is not to portray myself as 'clergy' but as a brother who needs healing. I have been prayed for intentionally when issues have come up, battles are being waged – basically to guard my heart and bring me through more whole than before the battle started. I have had ungodly inheritances from my family line prayed out and cast out. Past wounds have been dealt with. I receive general prayer ministry frequently, aiming for it at least once each week. I do journaling to listen to God as I seek to make sense of what is happening in my life. I have had some great peer support over the years, from people wise in areas where I have not had insight. Basically I believe there is no lack in the church for what we need to be whole so that our leadership is wholesome.

▪ **Self understanding:** The more I have understood my call, my gifts, my strengths, the more I have become free. I can remember that I used to feel deeply uneasy when people would say things like: You are our shepherd. The implication was that I could play 'god' and then they'd be fine. Something inside wanted to shout out: Jesus is your shepherd. My job is actually to help connect you to him and help you listen for his voice and follow his lead. That is my leadership role. And together with the other leaders that God put with me, we would then, under Jesus, shepherd the sheep. Not to make them dependent upon us, but to encourage them to be dependent upon Jesus and interdependent with all those they are connected to in the church. There is mutual support in the church, each of us carrying the load that God gives to us and in turn being supported by those nearest to us in the Body. It is the unconnected ones who look only to some figure up front. That is something we consciously work against for the love of them and God.

But small things, like doing a Myers Briggs

personality type indicator test, suddenly helped me to understand why I struggled in some aspects of leadership as an introvert. Though God has healed some of the introversion and made me more of a people person than I was, this test helped to know what I could offer in the face of the many expectations which people have put upon me over the years. Simple things like knowing what my gifts are have been liberating too. And the recent study into the role of 'strengths' and completing a strengths finder exercise helps me to understand what my unique role is alongside others.

I will say more about this in a later chapter, when speaking more generally about how people discover their gifts. The crucial thing is to know how God has wired me up so that I am not trying to be like someone else, nor trying to do things for which I have no ability in order to please someone other than Jesus.

Knowing our gifts and knowing our strengths enables us to play to our strengths, and to be competent in the areas where God has made us competent. It also sets us free to share leadership with those who have gifts which complement our own. I love to see others moving in their gifts – especially gifts that I don't have! And when they have similar gifts, to see the unique way in which those gifts add to the whole while never competing with mine or anyone else's.

There are also crucial things like understanding

why God has called us to this particular leadership role in this church at this time and not some other church or time. We need a sense of focus in terms of what we put our energy into, what part God has called and gifted us for within the whole. We need to be clear about the vision for the church so that we defend the values and priorities that we give ourselves to. Try defining what you would be prepared to die for (eg kingdom values that you would not abandon to achieve your purpose, a goal that you would pay the ultimate price to achieve) – and what you choose to live for (eg what really excites you about where you are and the call upon your life). In fact the whole kingdom of God vision and our part in bringing the rule of God to earth, that is the life of heaven to this world as Jesus did, has sharpened for me what I and the church are about. I am much clearer and more confident to lead because of the personal vision I carry.

Clearly personal prophetic ministry has a great role in connecting us to God's heart. To be prayed for on an ongoing basis, plus some of the one off opportunities at leadership conferences, have enabled me to see something of the potential God has for me. God has not completed his work in us – and it won't be complete until we see Jesus face-to-face and the job gets fully done. We need to know how he sees us so that we can take hold of that for which Christ took hold of us (Phil 3).

VI
The Apostolic Leader

The foundational leaders, as Paul understood it, were the apostle and prophet. The interplay between these two gifts is important, as Mike Bickle has written. Prophets are not meant to lead. But they are there to help the apostle lead better.

The chief thing about the apostolic leader is their ability to discern, to have a broader perspective – and as one who is 'sent' – especially to keep the church missional. The prophet can bring correction but the apostle gives direction. Pastors, teachers and even evangelists cannot give this leadership.

The apostolic gift checks to see if the church is losing its focus, or if it has got lost on one focus and no longer holds together the mission (to the world) and ministries (within the church) that make the church healthy.

This is illustrated so well by the events in Acts 6, where the first recorded dispute could have derailed the church's forward momentum. There was a food distribution crisis, but the apostles, instead of diverting their focus onto an internal issue, delegated the resolving of the problem to a team of anointed leaders. And the apostles held to their calling to keep to prayer and to the ministry of the Word of God. There is such a challenge here to those leaders who allow the crises to set the agenda for their ministry rather than keep to the agenda of leading. Gordon MacDonald and Eugene Petersen have written on this subject. What is clear to me is that if I allow the crises to set the agenda for ministry, Satan will keep sending them. When I work out what is urgent and what is important in ministry, and when I work out what crisis I must personally address and what I must require someone else to address, and when I make wise decisions about what time to give to a crisis so that important work also gets priority, *then* I am exercising apostolic leadership.

And apostolic leadership is there to keep the balance in the Body. We have all lived with passionate leaders who think the church should only exist for social justice or even to address environmental issues. The apostles must keep the main thing the main thing and ensure that the gospel of the kingdom is our central agenda and see that the many expressions of it are held together.

Another thing that we constantly battle with in the church are those who are so devoted to their ministry that those who do not join them are seen to be disobedient. *Why are you not like me?* is the question in their minds, if not actually on their lips. The whole world is judged according to such individual's own awareness of reality. The evangelist genuinely believes that if you are not leading another person to faith regularly, you are backsliding. The apostle values and honours all ministries and helps the Body to honour one another. The apostle sees the church through a wider lens and values the diversity, giving value to all the gifts in their place. And so the apostle is the one who brings balance when at the church meeting someone stands up and berates the church for their failure to care for the poor (in the way that *they* do!) or to pray like they do. We inevitably measure others in the church by our own calling and passion. The apostle is there to acknowledge what each brings and to guard the sensitive from false guilt.

The apostle is there to field the distractions and to keep the church on course. Apostolic leaders are the bearers of the vision, the keepers of the call given to that church. Often challenges come from the newest members, who want us to be like the church they left, or want a place to continue to play a role that they have left behind in another place. I am not one of those people who believe that the church should try to straightjacket people into a limited number of options for serving. But part of the role of the apostolic leadership is to ensure that the church does not get recruited to serve someone's passion. And I do not think a new person should be given space to lead anything (they can play on the team but not be captain) until they have settled down into our life, taken on our DNA and proved that they will submit themselves to what God is doing here.

In this, the apostolic leader particularly watches over the values that guard the life entrusted to the church. These values should be articulated. These are the measure by which we assess that we are being true to what God has called us to be. The biggest reversal in our life in the church where I was last a leader came from a conflict of very fundamental values. I believe it was an attempt by Satan to destroy the unique calling God had given to us and equipped us to live out. As a leadership we failed to address it, and part of the failure was due to conflicted loyalties to people instead of to values. If we'd had the values in place before the events, the path through the dark would have been a lot simpler.

The missional or apostolic call is critical to keep the church missional. It is so easy for the church to exist for itself – for everything we do to be for us. At times the apostle has to be pioneering. We are the ones who help to put energy into something that is lacking in the life of the church. Apostles initiate, not on our own but alongside others whom God has given to us to shift things forward.

Because of the pioneering nature of apostolic leadership, it will be inclined to get behind those with entrepreneurial gifts and will invest alongside them in taking up new callings, new risks, fresh vision.

It will bless what God stirs up. It will resource new ventures, and will make space for more than we have done up to now. I sense that this kind of leadership can handle complexity and diversity, due to the varieties of gifts that God raises up in each church. I often think that my task is to provide the covering under which people can follow their calling and find fulfilment in working with God where I would never work. A key role of apostolic leadership must be to help people find their place to serve – so it both releases and empowers each and every member of the Body.

*

Example of a Statement of Values

1. WORD BASED
    - We believe the scriptures to be the authoritative word of God
    -

2. GOD FOCUSED
    - Worship has a high value in our corporate life
    - We express our dependence in prayer

3. SPIRIT EMPOWERED
    - God empowers us to advance his kingdom in signs and wonders

4. SALVATION
    - Through faith in the cross of Jesus alone we are born again and reconciled to God

5. ACTIVE IN FAITH
    - For ourselves: believing that God can transform us into the likeness of Jesus
    - For the world: reaching out to the community in evangelism and good works
    - We give priority in our ministry to those who are generally marginalised, especially the poor and the young
    - Every member ministry

VII
Leader of Leaders

This is the place for the senior team, the elders. If we are to avoid being chaplains, we are to take up the call to release and resource leaders. Our ministry is to be chiefly to leaders. By all means keep our hand in in terms of the gifting we have – but the focus is to model leadership and help others whom God is calling to leadership, to grow as leaders. I can remember years ago someone saying that the fruit of the true leader is to produce leaders. We reproduce after our own kind. So the more we do it, the more others will also do it. The task of every leader is to disciple another leader out of the team that is being built to serve in an area of ministry. When we release leaders to lead in their place, they in turn also release others and share their leadership with the next generation of leaders.

We are trainers not players; coaches not front rankers. If the bulk of our ministry to people is not to leaders, we must refocus. The team needs us so that they can get better.

Being slightly removed, we will be most helpful to others closer to the work. We have to help them reflect; be sounding boards to test out their thoughts, their problem solving skills; and keep them from slipping into maintenance mode. This is always the default position of the church; because people are busy, maintaining what we are already doing may seem as if it's all we have energy for. But often new energy comes from new vision, the opening of opportunities, the enlisting of fresh passion. I am sometimes able to suggest that the leader has a conversation with a certain person who said something which now connects with what I am hearing at this moment. It is as if God has made me party to something he is stirring in someone else – and I see a link with this gap, or this work, and so I complete the link. I don't know if this is true for others, but when we have a love and a passion for the people God has given us to serve, he enables us to register and recall things that matter to him. We put together those whom God is calling to the same task or ministry.

Empower

It is very easy to disempower other leaders if we lack this awareness. As church leader, there are some traditional people in the parish whose expectation is that I will visit them or another member when they are in hospital. The day I choose to fulfil that expectation is the day I run the risk of disempowering the anointed ministry of all the lay people who are far more pastoral than I am. I have to let people know that they are better off if the pastors take care of them rather than the leader doing so. I have to honour the gifts that God has given to the Body and allow them to be promoted and not displace them.

Here is another instance: the leader who had oversight for our church cell groups was disappointed because he had called a meeting of cell group leaders and had a fifty percent attendance. He needed to meet with them again to do some training and share direction with them. He wanted me to issue the invitation. They will come if you summon them, was his thinking. But if I yielded to this, his leadership would have been emasculated. The authority had been given to him and it was up to him to *make it work*. My job was to help him do that and not do it instead of him.

So real authority must be given to the leaders. They make the call. And they in turn are to release authority and permission to everyone on the ground – so that people are able to make the call in the place of need. By the time people refer back for permission, the moment has passed, and they and the person in need are the poorer.

We do expect our leaders to report on what they are doing, the initiatives that they are following. And it is my task, along with the other elders to make ourselves aware. If something works against our values or our vision, we will engage with the leaders to work out how to bring it back on track.

But it is low control and high accountability. Real responsibility and authority must be delegated otherwise it is not true delegation. I have to relinquish control to the other person if they are going to be able to do anything with what has been entrusted to them. It is not my job to release someone to serve in an area and then attempt to control them to do it as I would have done it. Nor is it my job to foist upon them my vision for their work. Yes, they must fit within the overall vision of the church. And I can share my vision for what I see in their space but only to help them see more than they might have seen and, by the perspective I share with them, help them fit better into the whole church. But I also need to listen to their vision, what they see and why they believe God has called them. And, especially where they have more obvious gifting than mine, I want them to follow God's lead and grow the ministry as they use their gifts. In my mind, they must 'own' the ministry under God. It is their task to follow him and grow it as he leads.

And because ministry becomes more focused, it develops far more strongly than when one person is trying to balance a whole lot of different ministries. Some ministries led by creative people who put energy into what they are doing actually grow 'like Topsy', moving into areas we could never have seen from the centre. Opportunities open up on the ground – and those who minister must follow God. Leaders are there to check that things are not getting sidetracked.

It is our task to honour what God is doing through our teams. We acknowledge and commend what we see reported by responding to the leader concerned. We celebrate it in our elders meeting and give the feedback. God gives vision with his call. And the more people focus on what they are entrusted to lead, the more they will see the God-potential and the more they will deepen and extend the work.

As I have mentioned, at our church, we only employ to release ministry by the church. I can remember articulating this principle when we employed our first children's ministry worker. We were struggling to find someone to head up a key ministry. This is a growth engine for the church. Young families want to know that a church has a good ministry for their children so that church is a fun place to come to. We realised that we needed to employ someone who could handle all the organisational burden and recruit a team of volunteers to take on the interface with the children on Sunday morning. The worker then could establish a team of leaders to work alongside them – to be a sounding board, and to help oversee the staff of teachers, supporting and training them as they learn to lead their group of children. It was natural to employ such a person, so that we could open up this ministry to the many players we needed to recruit.

Succession depends upon people who come up through the ranks. The leader's job is to promote the next leaders. All ministry falters where it is carried by people in isolation: they get burnt out, they get stale, and worst of all, they exclude others from finding a place to serve.

The legacy we leave to the church is the leaders empowered by our leadership. A good leader will surround themselves with leaders who are more gifted and stronger than they. Everyone then gets to be better. I have grown by having strong leaders around me who help me to see what I am missing. They sharpen me and bless the church. The more we release others, the more we will see something of what Jesus saw: You will do greater things than these...

VIII
Servant of Servants

I heard someone say recently that they felt we should not have to emphasise that true leadership was 'servant leadership'. True leadership that works today is servant leadership. And it is to Jesus that the world owes a debt for changing the paradigm. Even in the world of business, the leaders who succeed are those who empower the team, not those who lord it over them (to quote Jesus). It is distressing when in the church the leader is less of a reflection of Jesus the Servant than in the secular world. In the more traditional churches we sadly see some monarchical bishops who do not submit power to those around them. It is so easy for leaders to misuse the power they hold and wield it to destroy and disempower and punish those who challenge them. Such leaders are in it for themselves. At a relational level they allow nothing to counter balance their power. John Stott once wrote that the bishops are the servants of the clergy and the clergy are the servants of the laity – and the laity have a servant problem!

But it is no less true in the newer churches. It is the spiritual language that enables us to elevate our power and control. If 'God has told me' then I put myself in an infallible position. The Bible seems to indicate that when God speaks, that is prophecy, and all prophecy should be tested. That is the point of shared leadership. It is to temper the abuse of power which flows from our fallen nature.

It is true that power does corrupt us. And it all has its links with titles and labels. 'Father knows best' is a line heard in many communities where the cleric likes to be called thus. It is clearly contrary to the words of Jesus, who longed for his followers to develop a kingdom culture under the only leader safe enough to be all powerful: the One True Lord Jesus Christ.

> But you are not to be called 'Rabbi' for you have one teacher and you are all brothers. And do not call anyone on earth 'father' for you have one Father and he is in heaven. Nor are you to be called instructors, for you have one Instructor, the Messiah. The greatest among you will be your servant. For those who exalt themselves will be humbled, and those who humble themselves will be exalted (Matthew 23:8-12).

For our generation, he could also have said: You are not to be called 'pastor' for you have one Shepherd who alone is good and safe.

The very titles exalt. The titles separate us from the Body and seduce us into believing that we and our calling are superior to the calling of our brothers and sisters.

But worse than that, people also will assign significance to us. And the longer we lead in the same church, the more weight and respect we attract. This can be a real frustration to people like me when I fail to pick up people's insecurities and learn via someone else that I left someone in a heap because I questioned something, or made an assumption and spoke from that place. I forget that not everyone is confident enough to challenge me in return – and I have to learn to temper my style and be more aware. All the time it is our task to work against a default setting, especially in older people or people conditioned by the church that formed them, that gives to us what only belongs to God.

In the kingdom of God there is no clergy/lay divide, no amateur/professional distinction. Everyone who is born again of water and the Spirit is a priest of the kingdom and in the church. None of us can do God's work without God. His presence and anointing is the only equipping we need to partner him in the extending of his kingdom. Ordination is purely recognition – it does not give what we don't have. And everyone's lack is God's opportunity. He is the one who gives everyone what they need and he does so without favouritism.

By choice, I now would never even wear a 'clerical-collar' or any badge of office which in any way lifts my ministry to a place of more significance than any other ministry. In the kingdom, the only ministry that counts is the ministry of Jesus, in which each one of us plays our own significant part. So no gift and no call is superior to another because they are all part of his work which he graciously shares with us.

I often think: It is so good not to have to be God to the church! It is not a role I am up to – even if others want me to take it on. To be a servant of God and of his people is a really liberating role. It does not mean that we become a doormat. It does not mean we are even to be treated as servants by those we serve. Leadership deserves honour and respect but we only receive that when we serve and not when we lord it over others.

We Wash Feet

The foot washing ministry of Jesus is underlined by the words he speaks: 'Now that I, your Lord and teacher have washed your feet, you also ought to wash one another's feet' (John 13:14). It is about many things, but for me it addresses the attitude I have towards others. If I am impatient with them, if I believe I know better or am better than them, if I do not trust them enough to risk releasing them, if I feel a need to instruct rather than suggest, then I need to stop looking down on them and ask myself: How do I serve them? How do I lift them up? How do I help them be more than they are? How do I help them discover the potential that God has placed within them? I look to lift and not to impose. I look to their feet to serve them and not to their head to speak down to them. That is a foot washing attitude that ministers to them as God does. It is being a leader that empowers.

Part Three

Practical Ways Forward

IX
Work with What You Have

I have had a dream all through my paid ministry that one day I would lead a church where there was a trumpet player. There is something stirring – and even portentous – about the trumpet sound, heralding the return of Jesus. We once had a player offer himself to us for two weeks while the orchestra he played with was in town for some production, but never anything lasting.

This dream has taught me that we cannot run the church on 'what ifs'. It is those God has given to us that present opportunities. To be continually bemoaning our lack is a dead end dream. We must live in the reality and see what we actually have. The call of God to your church will lie in their hands and yours. You might even have to start as far back as we did in one congregation we led in a daughter church. It was apparent that only two couples actually knew for sure that they were Christians and why that was so. Some of the others had a kind of faith that had been picked up by some sort of spiritual osmosis. They could have picked up all sorts of death as well, but God is good. God had told us simply to preach 'Jesus' and see what he did. We had a number of reactions. One dowager asked me one morning what had happened to God since all they heard about was Jesus. I asked her if Jesus was not God. She probably thought 'not quite' but did not take me on.

God then began to send us more and more Christians who added their testimony to ours. And then they began to urge a mission – and so it all unfolded. And God did a mighty work there. That congregation subsequently became a parish in its own right. It was a very gifted and spiritually willing church and was a great encouragement to us.

Faithful in a Little, Entrusted with Much

There is more to this. God has an amazing way of growing people's gifts and ministry. The testimony has always been there. Look at Acts 6. Seven men, 'known to be full of the Spirit and wisdom', were put forward as an answer to a dispute over the distribution of food. The book of Acts gives us a little insight on just two of these seven. Stephen became the first martyr of the church, not because of his ministry to widows but because he became a serious apologist. The inference must be that he practised on the widows! He had conversations with those he served, and then grew out of that experience. It is possible that those who were 'complainers' (v 1) may not have been saved – though I know some Christians who have not learnt that lesson after many years of following Jesus, despite warnings of Paul in 1 Corinthians 10! But with a need to persuade people to move into a true discipleship, Stephen cut his teeth. Before long he is 'full of God's grace and power', performing 'great wonders and signs...' and beginning to take on the theologians 'who could not stand up against the wisdom the Spirit gave him as he spoke.' This all started with distributing food. Never underestimate what God can do with a person who has a gift of hospitality and a listening ear and a heart with some conviction in it.

And Philip was one of the seven as well, the only person the Bible calls 'The evangelist.' He went off to Samaria and was used mightily before God removed him and took him into the desert to save a man from Ethiopia, thus taking the gospel beyond the Middle East. We also know that he had three daughters who were prophets. A godly heritage began when a young man helped to hand out food.

So I am saying: look out at who you have. Start asking God where to start and then invite the person into serving somewhere. Get them praying about whether God is calling them, otherwise they will be doing it for you and not for God. I will say a little more on this in the next chapter. Pray for them with the laying on of hands for an anointing for the ministry to which God has called them (Acts 6) and walk with them until they can run. As I have said before, they must have ownership. They must make the decisions, find the plan, listen for the vision.

What is apparent from Acts 6 is that people only begin to move into what might turn out to be a life work by starting somewhere. As Jesus put it: 'Those who are faithful in a little will be entrusted with much.' Here is the principle I have seen unfold time and time again. And not only with individuals but also with ministries. As people begin to collaborate, they begin to see so much more than what got them going in the first place. They see more and risk more.

So get people started. Get them to do the 'little' so they will move towards the 'much'.

Adequacy Never Built the Kingdom

We look within instead of looking up! I love the way Paul puts it in Romans 12, in his urging that we should not think of ourselves more highly than we ought (v 3). I seldom, if ever, find this a problem. Most people initially lack the belief that they can do anything. We must help them to begin to realise that they have already been enlisted when they yielded to Jesus as Lord, and that when he calls them, he knows better than they do what they have been prepared for. And in God's economy, nothing in our lives is ever wasted. Our life, even before our conversion, equips us for those God sends across our path. And as he does to Moses, to Joshua, to the disciples in the great commission in Matthew, he makes only one promise: I will be with you. My presence will go with you...

God does not call us and then send us off on our own. We never work *for* God. We only ever work *with* him. The Holy Spirit is a person – not some deposit of power that we run with until it runs out. We partner with God, and in fact he not only goes with us, he has already gone before us. He is at work in lives and situations long before we saw a need or an opportunity. He invites us to come along with him and join in with what he is doing. And everything we need is in him.

Work with what you have. The gifts and ministries you

need for today are present already in those God has given to you. Start with one and allow a testimony to rise up so that a momentum of change begins.

X

Ministry Comes from a Calling

One of the challenges of working with volunteers is that they can volunteer themselves out like they volunteered themselves in. And this is the problem with the church when it twists people's arms to rescue a ministry. We need to sustain or set up ministry to children – so we send out the press gang. It is far better to leave gaps than force people into them. Often God can only call people when the gap is left open. If we fill it, we mess up God's plan with someone he wanted to bring into play.

Leaders have to walk with God in this because God calls people. And our task as leaders is to learn to listen for prophetic words about who and when. And then we invite people to test their calling, encouraging people to pray about it. It is so crucial that people understand that they have been commissioned by God and that they answer to him. Or else somewhere along the line they get offended by something and then want to dump everything and run. It is as if people feel they do not own what they lead.

Ask any leader – much leadership is about helping people to deal with offence and start to grow through it. And often it is offence with the leader over them: We did not notice;

we did not compliment; they picked up something disapproving from us; or we were short with them.

I have a friend who says: 'If I have hurt you please tell me. And if you have hurt me please tell me because I wouldn't know that either!' Yes, let's ask God to deepen our sensitivity to one another.

But let us also seek to grow in our identity in God so that we have the relationship with him to deal with hurt. We do not have the luxury, as leaders and servants of God ourselves, of staying offended and taking our hurt out on God's servants, who are not our servants (Romans 14:4). Anyone with unhealed hurts will damage the church even if they are gifted.

But if we are answerable to God, when the reverses happen, it keeps throwing us back on to him. This is not the time to give up but the time to press on and push through into a deeper obedience. As Elder we are there to help the leader hang in until they have fulfilled their call *and* ensured their succession.

It deepens a sense of ownership of that which God has called us to. This is mine to walk with God until it is done. I heard a good phrase recently describing ministry as an art and not a science. That is how we need to see it. Ministry will be shaped by each minister and each leader. We are the artists under God's hand opening up God's working in lives and groups. God will take the uniqueness of each person to embody vastly different expressions of care, of teaching, of leading.

That is why any assumption in the mind of the person

that they must do the ministry to please the leader, or do it in a particular way because that is how someone else did it, is inevitably shown to be fallacious.

Train on the Job

Wimber and others have reminded us that Jesus trained by having people observe him, then work with him and then take personal responsibility for doing it. I do not know about you, but I have been on endless evangelism courses but I am still not one of those people who engages everyone next to me on the aeroplane before we have taken off. I believe that introverts tackle ministry differently from extroverts, but courses are much more a one size fits all, often aimed at making 'everyone like this'. And if they do not connect with who we are, they are a waste of time and resources.

The best way for people to learn is to assess themselves. People can thank me for a sermon, but I generally have an idea about whether God was able to use it or not. And so the role of the leader or mentor is to help the person become more aware through reflection; to encourage them to try fresh approaches; to help them discover ways to improve and extend what they do, to be more effective.

This is when the course finds its place: it is for those already involved in ministry. I find that I do now benefit from attending Willowcreek's Global Leadership Summit because I am always wrestling with questions around leadership. A counselling course will sharpen and stretch those who are already in a counselling ministry. A worship course will help worship leaders. What I am saying is that people are to be encouraged to try some 'work on the ground' before we send them off on training.

God grows us on the job. I have grown as a leader by leading. The more I reflect, especially with someone else who is working as I do, the more I stumble on to God's next thing. With the gifting from God, there also comes vision for ourselves and for the work that God has put in our hands. The more we engage with it and with him, the more things become clear, the more possibilities we see, the clearer we become about where God wants to take something.

Each Minister is Unique

You can have ten pastors on a team but they will all see things and do things differently. This is part of the amazing creativity of God. Different people can reach more people, serve more people, connect with more people, *because* of their differences. Different people meet different needs in us. This is the glory of the Church, the Body, and the diversity by which God expresses his glorious life.

And God will give each person a vision for their ministry – that is how faith operates in our gifts: God stretches us and grows us into the minister that he sees us to be long before we see for ourselves. So as we grow others into ministry the last thing that we should do is control them or want them to do something 'my way.' Rather, we should be encouraging them *not* to copy us but to follow God's creative Holy Spirit and express the life of Jesus in its fullness together with us. The gift might be the same but it is shaped by each minister under God to create God's masterpiece.

We are to help them to respond to God and not just report to us.

XI
Discovering Gifts

There are many ways for people to be helped to know which direction to move in. Some processes are mechanical and help us to recognise what we are already doing. Some are by prophetic revelation as people ask God to show us what gifts he has put into a person's life.

For some people the challenge is: are these 'spiritual gifts' or natural? What is apparent from Paul is that in terms of spiritual (supernatural) gifts, God the Holy Spirit can distribute any gift to anyone in any situation where the gift is needed – all gifts to all people as God wants them deployed (1 Corinthians 12:11). We are encouraged to have faith about receiving the supernatural equipping God needs us to have in that moment. With the other gifts, initially they can be natural, but under the Holy Spirit they become anointed and *life giving* as He operates through us. So a person can have a natural leadership gift which under the Holy Spirit increases in capacity to shepherd and establish a group that is not just about the 'natural'. It will establish a people of God under God. It is the operation of the Holy Spirit in the gift which makes the natural supernatural.

*

Self Awareness

But in our creation, God has uniquely endowed us with abilities and put a heart in us to see the world in a particular way. One of the most helpful exercises I did early on in this unfolding of how the church is gifted was an exercise relating to motivational gifts (see summary at end of chapter). This exercise is based on Paul's list of gifts in Romans 12. These are natural capacities whether or not we are ever born again into God's family. So you can do this exercise with everyone. People listen to the description of how people operate naturally in response to need and then score themselves on a scale of 1-10 for each of the seven gifts (prophecy, serving, teaching, encouraging, giving, leading, mercy). In order to get people to discover their gifting, I require everyone to mark their strongest gift at 10. I am no longer amazed at how people are reluctant to score themselves with a number that makes them appear to be blowing their own trumpet. There is such a robbing of potential in people who are far quicker to believe they can't than that they can. But they are gifts – which, yes, we may not yet be using but we mostly know in our hearts.

What is revealed can have a life-changing impact on us. One young person in our church went back and resigned her job and registered at university to do a teaching diploma because she realised that she was not flowing in her life gifts. My wife suddenly came to terms with her dominant gift of prophecy which up to that point she had fought because of her natural ability to see through people and their motives with an accuracy that she found uncomfortable and negative.

She came instead to accept her gifting and learn how to use what God had given her for his sake. How we need the prophetic in the church!

Prophetic Discernment

When God began to restore the prophetic gift more widely in the church, initially it was seen in prophetic words being offered in times of worship both in small groups or in the church congregation when assembled. Then we began receiving words of knowledge as we prayed in preparation to minister healing in the church or while we prayed with people for healing.

But then we began to understand how the gift was not given just for problems but to release people into callings (see Acts 13), to experience a deeper sense of God's love for them. This is the key understanding of the test for prophecy in the New Testament which Paul uses in 1 Corinthians 14 (v 3) to strengthen, encourage, comfort and (v 31) instruct. And so we practised how to hear God for one another in small groups of three, listening for what God might be saying to each person. I have also done this in places like home cells, where we affirmed each other by what gifts we valued in each other. And as we did this God seemed to show us more about each other than we had yet seen.

The experience which for me was most life changing was when attending a leaders' course at St Andrew Chorleywood in 1995. It was at that point called a Hensol Retreat but subsequently was renamed as a New Wine Retreat to line up with other ministry out of that church. All those on the retreat, plus the leaders ministering to us, waited on God for the Father's affirmation of each leader in turn. I was encouraged to take hold of what God made me to be and I began to move into a potential that I had been reluctant to embrace. It actually liberated and fulfilled me, opening up all sorts of life opportunities to me.

In Bethel Church, Redding, California they have sought to cultivate a culture where people learn to honour what God has revealed about someone even before this person begins to exercise their gift. It encourages the belief that God has gifted people beyond where we can yet see. So we seek to see them as God does and help release them into their life work and call.

Questionnaires

There are many useful questionnaires that have been drawn up to uncover for us where our giftings lie. *The Natural Church Development* material developed by Christian Schwartz is helpful, but for me, the broadness of Willowcreek's Network course seems to be the most helpful. It gets people connected to their passion, which points people in the direction in which a gift could be used. Suppose you have a prophetic gift but a passion for children; it is marrying these two that is the exciting thing. Every ministry needs prophetic input, and every ministry need administrative help. If we combine gift with passion we have a breadth of service that can keep a ministry functional and fresh.

And it also helps people to see where best to function in the church, encouraging them to consider issues such as whether they are people persons or task persons, structured or spontaneous. Knowing our gift is not enough: we need to find a place to play where it works for us and others so that God can use us to the maximum. Doers should never sit on committees – they simply get bored and lose motivation. They don't have to be at the meeting to learn what to do. They just need to be asked after the meeting is over!

APPENDIX

Motivational Gifts

In Romans 12:3-8 Paul lists seven gifts which are motivational – perhaps instinctive gifts for you. They are how God has 'wired you up' so that in particular situations you will respond/react according to who you are. Even before people come to faith, they will operate in these ways. It is about who they are, and whom God created them to be.

I will list the gifts, with a description of their purpose and function, then share a story that was told by the first person who taught these things to me (Charles Gordon). The task you need to undertake, which will help to focus you on your natural gifting, will be to find the one gift that most truly describes how you act instinctively – which gift describes you; the gift for which you score ten out of ten. And then score yourself on the other six gifts. It is good to know your second and third strongest, as well as your weakest gifts!

*

▪ **Prophetic gift**: Meets spiritual needs. A God-given ability to see through a person, a situation; to discern right motives and be aware of sin. Such a person often feels critical. And may fear not being taken seriously. A seer. Biblical example: John the Baptist Luke 3:3-20.

▪ **Serving gift**: Meets practical needs. A doer, who finds fulfilment in serving others. Task focused rather than people focused. Should not serve on committees. A 'let's stop talking about it and get on with the action' type. Biblical example: Martha Luke 10:38-42.

▪ **Teaching gift**: Meets mental needs. Imparts knowledge in a systematic and orderly way, clarifies truth. Enjoys research. Biblical example: Apollos Acts 18:24-28.

▪ **Encouragement gift**: Meets personal needs. Stimulates faith, provokes commitment, growth, achievement. Releases people into success. Biblical example: Barnabas Act 4:36 & 11:22ff.

▪ **Gift of Giving**: Meets material needs. A contributor who shares in ministry of others by support. Releases material assets. Responds to logic not emotion. Biblical example: Abraham Genesis 13 & 14.

▪ **Leadership gift**: Meets effectiveness needs.

Organiser, who co-ordinates, has vision, plans and administers. Delegates, empowers. Biblical example: Nehemiah.

- **Mercy gift**: Meets emotional needs. Laughs with those who laugh, weeps with those who weep. Feels with people; attracts those with inner troubles. Compassionate. Finds it hard to say 'No'. Biblical example: Good samaritan Luke 10:29-37.

Find Yourself in this Story

Joe was injured in a motor accident and landed up in hospital having to undergo surgery. The first person to arrive at Joe's bedside was the comforter (mercy gift). As Joe was regaining consciousness and groaned, the comforter groaned. Every time Joe ached, the comforter ached.

The server arrived after a day or so and said: 'Hi Joe. What can I do for you? Let me get you a soft pillow. Any tasks needing to be done at home?'

The prophet arrived next and asked Joe: 'What were you doing to land up here?'

It wasn't long before the teacher turned up, with a Bible under his arm. After a short connecting conversation, he offered to share with Joe a passage in the Bible he felt would be applicable to him. It would only take an hour.

The exhorter arrived and said: 'Hey, Joe, isn't God great? Just look at the opportunity he has given you to witness to the nurses and doctors – and a mission field of patients right here in the room with you. Isn't God good?'

The administrator (leader) did not even go to see Joe. He phoned the ward to find out when Joe would be released because Joe was needed for a meeting coming up soon.

The giver, knowing Joe was going to be in some kind of financial embarrassment, arrived the day before his discharge and settled the hospital account.

So, which one were you?

XII
Structure to Release

When you read Paul's description of the Body in 1 Corinthians 12 and Ephesians 4, it reminds us life passes where there is connection, at the joints. And we are talking 'body', not just a picture of a random 'head' with digits attached only to the head as in some grotesque monster. Imagine if all the ministers/members only functioned in relation to the head, whether that means Jesus or the local pastor: the former would look like anarchy, everyone doing their own things for God; and the latter would be designed to test the capacity of the local pastor to the limit so that he could only release into ministry as many as he could personally manage. Further, it must be obvious that even the foot or the hand has many component parts that all function together to achieve mobility and dexterity for purposeful action.

So the church needs to develop some sort of structure so that people can easily find a place to function. It needs to be a structure which releases ministry and does not seek to control it. It should be there to support and enhance, to extend and develop capacity to serve, not just the church but also God's world: A structure which is missional, offering to the community the resources of heaven which we enjoy so freely in the church; and a structure which releases resources into the church as well, so that all grow up into the fullness of the stature of Jesus. So it needs to be flexible enough to release a limitless number of ministers and missionaries – as many as belong within the local church. God sent us a retired cleric once who had wanted to come to us when he had first retired, but because so much was going on he assumed he would not be needed. So he offered himself to another church but did not feel fulfilled and so came to us. We grabbed hold of him - and he and his wife have been able to add enormously to our life. Anyone who puts up their hand is snapped up. The kingdom vision is enormous. We are preparing the world for the return of our King. I have yet to be in a church where one extra person was not needed. In fact, our greatest challenge is how to raise the percentage of members involved in ministry – how to move them from being spectators to players.

The process by which our church came to where we are arose simply from a planning meeting where we identified focus areas that we wanted to address to strengthen the life of the church. Having determined eight areas to focus on, we closed our home cells for a month and encouraged people to meet in those focus areas with others who shared their passion – whether for children and youth ministry or for pastoral care; whether for evangelism or social concern. We tasked each of the eight groups to work out what they believed we should do as a church in each of those areas in order to become the church God wanted us to become. They worked on a vision and some actions to achieve the vision. Then for eight weeks, each group in turn was given our Sunday services with which to share their dream and their plan. We abandoned our preaching for eight weeks! But God stirred life as people spoke about what God had provoked in them. We encouraged people who were caught by what was shared to offer themselves to the team who had shared, so that they could join up with each team who would work to fulfil what God was showing us. In fact, those who took responsibility to present to the congregations revealed gifts of leadership and communication we had never noticed before. It was an exciting and creative time.

Home cells resumed but the ministry areas met less frequently (monthly at first) to move their plans forward. Some really good ministry began to happen and lay people found a place to play for God. Some ministry floundered. At times it was the quality of the leadership, at others it was simply the time restraints that competent leaders lived with, which prevented them from giving the energy and space that pioneering requires.

What became apparent was that leadership is key to any structure. There are never enough leaders. And some people put their hand up to lead but lack the gifting; they end up taking everything into their own hands and then burn out, leaving a whole area of ministry uncovered because everyone else has signed off because they were not being given space to serve.

So the structure needs to support leaders. But as an elder – by that I mean that my role as a leader of leaders – is not to be a foreman but an empowering person. I am there to help bring light into difficult areas, to suggest where things are being overlooked or opportunities are not being exploited. This puts pressure upon the leader to be someone who has things to offer, things to give. So a key responsibility of the leader is to take care of self. If I need help, I must know where to find it. If I need resources, I must learn what resources me. If I need feeding, I must learn to feed myself. I cannot blame anyone else for the state of my life if I am a leader. A leader ultimately must know how to feed themselves, not moan that others have not fed them. What helps is to gather other leaders around; this, as we have seen, helps with succession, with breadth of vision and creativity in the face of problems. The New Testament pattern for leadership is always at least in pairs and even in teams.

Because ministry tends to grow like Topsy, the eight focus areas soon became sixteen, and then more as people became more focused into specific areas of need. Initially we had every leader on our eldership team but the quality of our leadership overall dropped. We tended to micro-manage at that level and lost sight of the bigger picture and the gaps that were not being covered. We were managing what we were doing but not seeing what we weren't doing.

So we pared our leadership of the ministry down to six (now seven elders) who oversaw groups of ministry. The structure of this leadership appears below.

The task of the elders is to stop ministry from getting bogged down, to keep an eye on leaders (caring, releasing, empowering) and to help the whole church keep moving forward into God's purposes.

Elders

Elders are those that head up groups of ministries, those who hold the whole leadership together, leading the ministry leaders. Below is a list of roles and responsibilities we have found conducive to our aims.

- Leadership and Discipleship Elder: Growing leaders, and training and discipleship in the church.

- Church Community Elder: Growing our sense of belonging – and pastoral care. Communication.

- Social Justice Elder: outreach projects to empower and assist the disempowered.

- Spirituality Elder: Ministry of worship, prayer and Holy Spirit prayer ministry.

- Family life Elder: Ministry to families – marriage, parenting.

- Elder to the Young: Ministry to children, teens, young adults.

- Outreach Elder: Provoking the church to be outward looking and win people to Jesus.

XIII
People into Place

Shifting the church from a clergy-centred-ministry-model to an every-member-ministry-under-God- model is a constant challenge. We have church history to work against because for so long, other than a few practical serving roles, most people were excluded from wider ministry. So there is a whole process of re-education. And we live in an age of entertainment where many unchurched people are happy to come in and enjoy the show, assuming that they are not expected to do anything except put in an appearance.

Our church had some interesting feedback from a person who went on to become our youth pastor. When she first attended the church, she saw everything running amazingly (to her anyway!) and her first thought was that she was not needed and so perhaps should try another church. Fortunately she stuck with us, and then, because of the kind of person she was, she began to see the gaps. We had a prophetic picture given to us about this time which was simply of a diamond mesh fence. And because we had been grappling with drawing people into ministry, we came to see that God was telling us: to those on the outside the fence is a barrier, to those on the inside all we can see are the holes, gaps here and gaps there, gaps everywhere. We never have enough volunteers for what we have a vision for – and more than anything, we never have enough leaders to draw those with a heart to serve into a purposeful place to offer their gifts.

I have mentioned earlier that we resist paying for ministry. If we employ someone it is to enable the release of more volunteers by carrying the load, which makes serving possible for people who have busy and demanding work and home lives. So we carefully work against moving to a ministry model where no one serves unless they are paid to do so.

We have tried all sorts of ways to recruit people. Getting all our home cells to do the Willowcreek Network course, preaching into the material week by week, and then having a 'Market Day' where all our ministries put up displays on a Sunday at the end of the exercise. Those leading ministries staffed the displays, answered questions and got people to sign up to serve. One older member caught me as I was moving around watching the process with the words: 'Can we go out to play next week too?' People enjoyed it and it was quite a challenge to gather everyone back to complete our worship. And the marketers signed people up with passion.

We have had a celebration Sunday where we promoted our ministries, again with a chance at the end of worship to visit displays and engage with ministry leaders. We have had stewardship days where we have asked people to commit themselves to giving time to serve as well as make a financial commitment to the church's ministry.

Ministry leaders also need to be organised enough to take up the offers they get. We have had some real undermining of the climate of volunteering when people have offered themselves and never been followed up on. There is always a place alongside someone in the team, and team members need to have a vision to multiply what they do through others. If the team is not growing it will soon become depleted, so just as the church needs to keep growing because people die or move away, so ministries need to keep recruiting all the time. And everyone we bring in adds to the ministry on offer, adds to the mix, because each of us is unique. And we soon recognise that in time the new recruits may well take the ministry way beyond us and what we presently see as our calling.

We also take our new people through an evening of four commitments: A commitment to Transform (i.e. I am a work in progress and the church has resources for my healing and growth), Belong (I have to belong to the cell to feel that I belong to the whole), Serve (I have to find a place to serve so that I grow up into Jesus in faith and ministry), Resource (I will tithe my resources to the storehouse that resources me and serves our community). We have a list of ministry opportunities on a one-page hand out and invite people to make some commitment to be involved.

I believe the task of the leaders is to persevere until every Christian becomes alive in the Body – not to serve is to atrophy and die, and the consequent gangrene poisons the body. We are speaking about a culture change. The church needs no armchair critics but living sacrifices, laying down life for Jesus and his kingdom.

Ultimately it depends on ministers recruiting ministers. I know leaders who pray for God to show them whom to engage with, and then go up and invite those God points out to them to come and have a go at something. Just because we try something does not commit us for life; it allows people the freedom to search until they find God's place for them. Sometimes we can only discover our hearts by trying something and find a passion ignited by what we do.

I find that often in conversation it is possible to recognise a person's passion: the way they speak about something, the things that they always talk about… We could also be more proactive with those in our cell groups, getting them to share what ministry they are involved in and getting the group to pray for one another for their serving. This will change the culture at grass roots level and get people looking for their place to serve.

If someone senses that God is wanting them to begin some entirely new ministry, my first response is to get them to talk to the elder under whose oversight this ministry would naturally fall. And then to look for a partner to start the work. If God is in it he will have been calling someone else to be alongside them. The Elder may be able to suggest a person. Or else the pioneer minister should be asking God to lead them to the person he is raising to partner them. If nothing shifts perhaps they need to get some clarity from God about the ministry before God is able to put someone alongside them.

This is a ceaseless task for the leaders, but it is essential for the realisation of the goal of everyone serving so that the whole Body grows up into Jesus, our head.

XIV
Guard the Church

So much excellent material has been printed on the importance of character in gifting, but it needs repeating here.

We have seen many gifted people whose character and people skills make it difficult and at times even wrong to put them in a place decided upon solely in relation to their gifts. We have had young people that we have had to discipline for the sake of their own gifting and future potential. We have a role in guarding a life from overexposure so that with help the gift, the person and the church are safe.

There are many areas of danger, as Richard Foster reminded us in his book *Money, Sex and Power*.

The exercise of authority in a serving way is a protection from such danger. Having shared leadership also restrains some of the bad traits that could come to the fore in threatening situations (threat either to leader or led!) And developing an empowering leadership that risks using others rather than seeking to control others is a critical factor. It is often simply about security in our identity before God.

As a senior leader, I am one of those who at times has to have the difficult conversations with those whose lives are out of order. I am also willing to come alongside other leaders whom I oversee, to help them have the conversations that need to happen. If someone is thought to be involved in some immoral behaviour, or if there is a report of some form of abuse of leadership, we have to investigate. Damaging behaviour destroys, and Satan loves to mess with the lives of leaders so that he has access to the church through them.

If I behave immorally or abusively, I have sent a non-verbal permission to the whole church to behave in a like manner. If it is OK for him, it is OK for us. But even if my behaviour is completely hidden from view, I still open a spiritual door for Satan to range through the church – because I have opened a door into all those over whom I have influence and made them vulnerable because of my sin.

And God will not send people to us to care for because they would not be safe. And parents will remove their children from our youth group if they think that the leadership is not addressing the wolf we have placed over or among the lambs. And ministry teams will dwindle as gradually people remove themselves from a toxic or a dangerous or unsupportive team, or a team that cannot keep confidences.

It is far better to leave a ministry vacant and not operating than to place into leadership those who create a foothold for Satan. The church belongs to God – she is Jesus' bride. The shepherds are there to protect the flock.

It is not just the leaders who can destroy ministry. If there is one person who spoils it for everyone else, it is the leader's unhappy task to confront the destroyer to protect the work. I read a book recently that described handling the problem person on a team as like handling the child in the sandpit who throws sand into other people's eyes. It is the one who can cause all to lose heart. No one needs to confront it on their own: there are co-leaders or elders who are there to support the leaders. Two leaders meeting together with the one needing to be disciplined protects the leader and the one they are responsible for. We all share in this responsibility. I am grateful for the leaders who have joined me in some difficult conversations, and tempered my disciplining of others.

Some damage is simply done by unhealed people. People move into ministry out of a need to be needed. I have worked with many people in this position. They are unhealthy for the church and need to be confined lest they bring death instead of life to those they minister to. Hurting people often attract other hurting people – and they quickly become a gruesome twosome. Until I allow God to heal me I am mostly unable to help others. I do not have the faith to move you into the place that God still needs to take me.

Jesus ensured that Peter was properly restored after his resurrection (John 21) so that he ministered out of love for Jesus because he knew that Jesus first loved him. We have gifted but unhealed people who could be really useful – but they tend to leave people unhelped because they themselves are unhealed. They operate like lightning rods, attracting hurting people. They are often the focus of unhappiness in the church, but nothing changes for them or those who go to them. It is when we get healed that we have life to offer to those who are themselves hurting. We communicate life not death, because life has been restored to us.

Jesus himself had to face some of the temptations of ministry: Do I do this to feed myself? When I do it, is it about me putting myself on display so that I feed on the adulation? When I do it, is it about my power or is it a yielded servant power which seeks to empower and is unconcerned about wanting to be first? Am I attending to myself as well as to others (1 Timothy 4:16)?

I was once rebuked when someone referred to a particularly difficult time in my life as my *angry* phase! I was struggling with a rejection of my leadership and ministry from a faction of leaders in one congregation, and as I worked through with God whether to leave paid ministry and return to the world of business, I was initially in a very bad place. I probably should have taken a sabbatical and let God resolve things for me but I pressed on and did damage because I, myself, was damaged and unhealed.

There is no lack of resources in God to restore each of us. And we will not be whole until we see Jesus face to face and become like him 'because we will see him as he is' (1 John 3:2). So I am not saying that we should not minister or lead until we are whole! If we are committed to the transformation of ourselves through intimate worship (2 Cor 3:18) which enables us to encounter God, if we are receiving prayer regularly to allow God to refresh and restore us, if we get help from counsellors, prophetic prayer ministry or whatever it takes to hasten wholeness, I believe God undertakes for us. In fact, I believe that he cares for the church in spite of us because he loves us and loves those we serve.

Part Four

Kingdom Vision

XV
A Missional Church

I realise that for many people the church is an end in itself. We do things for the church. Our leadership is for the church. Our ministries are for the church.

This misses the whole point of why the Holy Spirit formed us into a church from Pentecost onwards, building on the community which had formed around the person and kingdom ministry of Jesus. The church and each Christian has been called to faith and community to advance the kingdom of God.

Isaiah has the picture of the reign of the Prince of Peace, of the increase of his government and peace there shall be no end (Isa 9:6 , 7). Paul has this vision of Jesus ascending 'in order to fill the whole universe' (Ephesians 4:10). This is not some sort of local or domestic endeavour in which we are engaged. As Bill Johnson and John Wimber and probably others have pointed out: Whatever stays inside the church dies, because the meeting place is the training place for the market place. I learn how to pray for someone's healing in the safety of the church alongside others who have walked longer and further than me, so that I can pray for healing in the office this week. I grow in my awareness of the gifts of revelation so that I can open up conversations and connect to God those who are far from him. God gives me influence in the market place so that I bring his kingly rule to those places, changing the culture to one of honour, of honesty, of truth, of righteousness and of love, so that people flourish in that space.

We assemble as a church (congregation or cell) to be built up so that we go out from our meeting as missionaries who are restoring God's rule where Satan has been working: killing, stealing and destroying. We have to catch this vision: that we are preparing the world of the return of the King!

And God has given us the resources of heaven to do this ministry. As Christians we must read the book of Acts prayerfully at least once a year and remind ourselves that it relays the pattern for us to follow. The kingdom of God advances in the power of the Holy Spirit. The kingdom is not a matter of talk but of power. If we talk, we need to know how to let God confirm his word by signs and wonders. Or do the signs and wonders, then follow up with words as Peter did in Acts 2 and 3 and on. Acts was just the starting point. In our generation, the task is to seek for the restoration of the church so that the next generation grows beyond us rather than lets it slip back into institutional powerlessness.

It took some years after I first heard John Wimber speak about the Great Commission in Matthew 28 before the penny really dropped for me. When Jesus tells the disciples to pass on to those they reach, 'teaching them to obey everything I have commanded you', he is referring to the missional commands. Yes, all the other commands about loving our enemies and loving our neighbours and loving one another will help the mission. But the pattern of Jesus in the gospels, and the church in Acts, was to advance the kingdom in power.

And the mission commands were to heal the sick, raise the dead, cast out demons, cleanse the lepers and preach the good news. Anything less than that is not going to do much in this postmodern age, in which people no longer ask if something is true and so propositions will not impress them. We need a demonstration of the King's power released through the cross and made available to us by the anointing of the Holy Spirit upon our powerless lives.

A church which expects everyone to minister and equips everyone to minister is a force to be reckoned with when we return to our mission field outside the building where we gather. This is the end point: the mobilising of God's people both for God's ministry and God's mission.